HAL LEONARD
Easy Pop Christmas Melodies

GUITAR METHOD
Supplement to Any Guitar Method

T0071699

INTRODUCTION

Welcome to *Easy Pop Christmas Melodies*, a collection of 15 Christmas favorites arranged for easy guitar. If you're a beginning guitarist, you've come to the right place; these well-known songs will have you playing, reading, and enjoying music in no time!

This collection can be used on its own or as a supplement to the *Hal Leonard Guitar Method* or any other beginning guitar method. The songs are arranged in order of difficulty. Each melody is presented in an easy-to-read format—including lyrics to help you follow along and chords for optional accompaniment (by your teacher, if you have one).

ISBN 978-1-4584-0796-2

HAL•LEONARD®
CORPORATION

7777 W. BLUEMOUND RD. P.O. BOX 13819 MILWAUKEE, WI 53213

Visit Hal Leonard Online at
www.halleonard.com

SONG STRUCTURE

The songs in this book have different sections, which may or may not include the following:

Intro
This is usually a short instrumental section that "introduces" the song at the beginning.

Verse
This is one of the main sections of a song and conveys most of the storyline. A song usually has several verses, all with the same music but each with different lyrics.

Chorus
This is often the most memorable section of a song. Unlike the verse, the chorus usually has the same lyrics every time it repeats.

Bridge
This section is a break from the rest of the song, often having a very different chord progression and feel.

Solo
This is an instrumental section, often played over the verse or chorus structure.

Outro
Similar to an intro, this section brings the song to an end.

ENDINGS & REPEATS

Many of the songs have some new symbols that you must understand before playing. Each of these represents a different type of ending.

1st and 2nd Endings
These are indicated by brackets and numbers. The first time through a song section, play the first ending and then repeat. The second time through, skip the first ending, and play through the second ending.

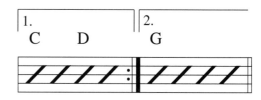

D.S.
This means "Dal Segno" or "from the sign." When you see this abbreviation above the staff, find the sign (𝄋) earlier in the song and resume playing from that point.

al Coda
This means "to the Coda," a concluding section in the song. If you see the words "D.S. al Coda," return to the sign (𝄋) earlier in the song and play until you see the words "To Coda," then skip to the Coda at the end of the song, indicated by the symbol: ⊕.

al Fine
This means "to the end." If you see the words "D.S. al Fine," return to the sign (𝄋) earlier in the song and play until you see the word "Fine."

D.C.
This means "Da Capo" or "from the head." When you see this abbreviation above the staff, return to the beginning (or "head") of the song and resume playing.

CONTENTS

SONG	PAGE
Good King Wenceslas	4
Jolly Old St. Nicholas	5
Away in a Manger	6
The Chipmunk Song	7
Caroling, Caroling	8
O Come, O Come Immanuel	9
Grandma Got Run Over by a Reindeer	10
Jingle Bells	12
A Holly Jolly Christmas	14
Do You Hear What I Hear	16
You're All I Want for Christmas	18
Let It Snow! Let It Snow! Let It Snow!	20
Silver Bells	22
Here Comes Santa Claus (Right Down Santa Claus Lane)	23
Santa Claus Is Comin' to Town	24

GOOD KING WENCESLAS

Words by JOHN M. NEALE
Music from Piae Cantiones

JOLLY OLD ST. NICHOLAS

Traditional 19th Century American Carol

AWAY IN A MANGER

Words by JOHN T. McFARLAND
Music by JAMES R. MURRAY

THE CHIPMUNK SONG

Words and Music by
ROSS BAGDASARIAN

CAROLING, CAROLING

Words by WIHLA HUTSON
Music by ALFRED BURT

O COME, O COME IMMANUEL

Plainsong, 13th Century
Words translated by JOHN M. NEALE
and HENRY S. COFFIN

GRANDMA GOT RUN OVER
BY A REINDEER

Words and Music by
RANDY BROOKS

Chorus

Grand-ma got run o-ver by a rein-deer

walk-ing home from our house Christ-mas Eve.

You can say there's no such thing as San-ta, but

To Coda

as for me and Grand-pa, we be-lieve.

Verse

1. She'd been drink-ing too much egg-nog
2., 3. *See additional lyrics*

and we begged her not to go.

But she for-got her med-i-ca-tion, and she

stag-gered out the door in-to the snow.

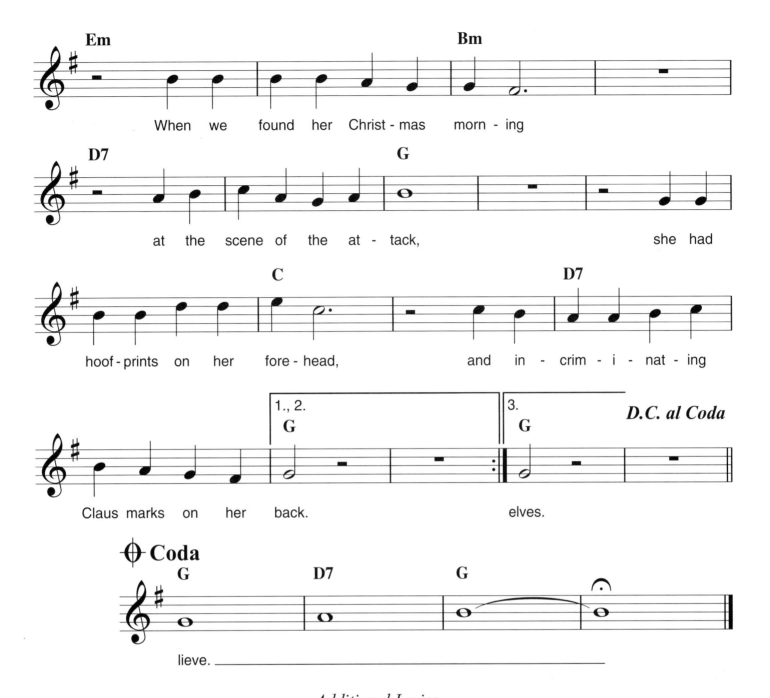

lieve. _____

Additional Lyrics

2. Now we're all so proud of Grandpa,
   He's been taking this so well.
   See him in there watching football,
   Drinking beer and playing cards with Cousin Mel.
   It's not Christmas without Grandma.
   All the family's dressed in black,
   And we just can't help but wonder;
   Should we open up her gifts or send them back?

3. Now the goose is on the table,
   And the pudding made of fig.
   And the blue and silver candles,
   That would just have matched the hair in Grandma's wig.
   I've warned all my friends and neighbors,
   Better watch our for yourselves.
   They should never give a license
   To a man who drives a sleigh and plays with elves.

JINGLE BELLS

Words and Music by
J. PIERPONT

Jin - gle bells,   jin - gle bells,   jin - gle all the

way.   Oh, what fun it is to ride in a

one horse o - pen sleigh! _____ Jin - gle bells,

jin - gle bells,   jin - gle all the way.

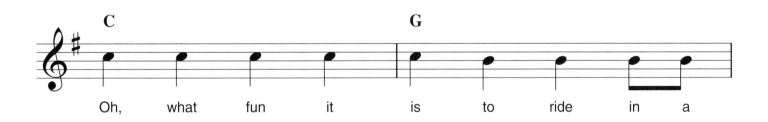

Oh, what fun it is to ride in a

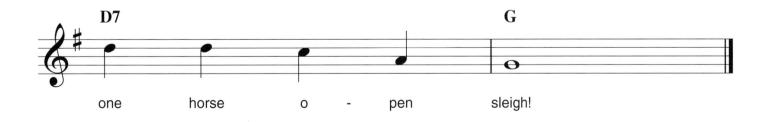

one horse o - pen sleigh!

A HOLLY JOLLY CHRISTMAS

Music and Lyrics by
JOHNNY MARKS

Verse

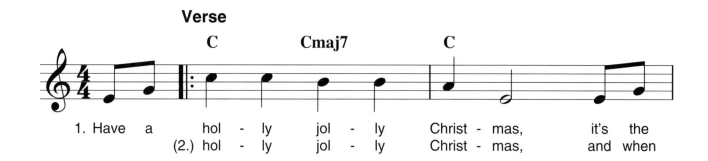

1. Have a hol - ly jol - ly Christ - mas, it's the
(2.) hol - ly jol - ly Christ - mas, and when

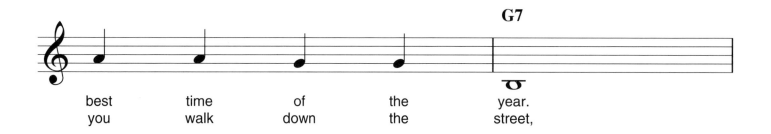

best time of the year.
you walk down the street,

I don't know if there'll be snow but
say hel - lo to friends you know and

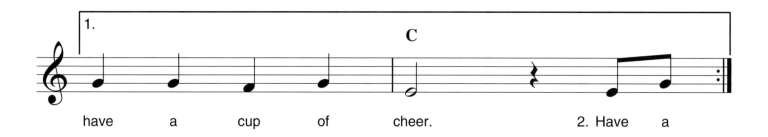

have a cup of cheer. 2. Have a

Bridge

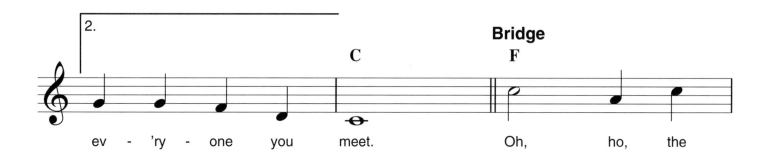

ev - 'ry - one you meet. Oh, ho, the

Em   F   C

mis - tle - toe   hung   where   you   can   see.

Dm   Am   D7

Some - bod - y   waits   for   you,   kiss   her   once   for

Outro

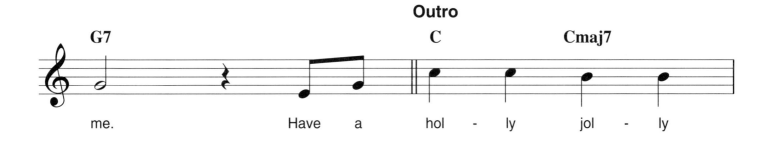

G7   C   Cmaj7

me.   Have   a   hol - ly   jol - ly

C   G7

Christ - mas,   and   in   case   you   did - n't   hear,

C

oh,   by   gol - ly,   have   a   hol - ly   jol - ly

D7   G7   C

Christ - mas _____   this   year. _____

DO YOU HEAR WHAT I HEAR

Words and Music by NOEL REGNEY
and GLORIA SHAYNE

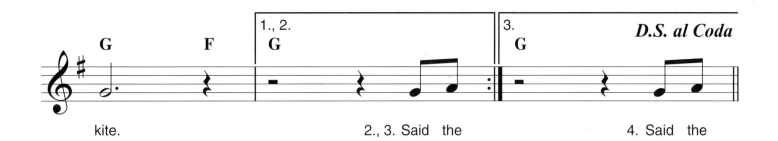

kite.   2., 3. Said   the   4. Said   the

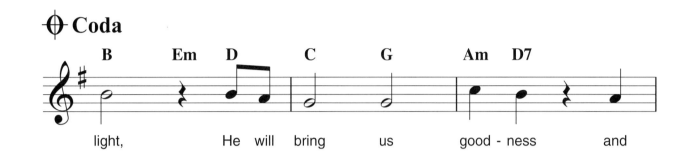

light,   He   will   bring   us   good - ness   and

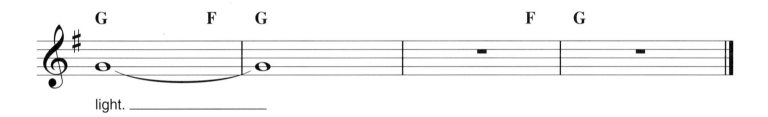

light. _____

Additional Lyrics

2. Said the little lamb to the shepherd boy,
   Do you hear what I hear?
   Ringing through the sky, shepherd boy,
   Do you hear what I hear?
   A song, a song, high above the tree,
   With a voice as big as the sea,
   With a voice as big as the sea.

3. Said the shepherd boy to the mighty king,
   Do you know what I know?
   In your palace warm, mighty king,
   Do you know what I know?
   A Child, a Child shivers in the cold,
   Let us bring Him silver and gold,
   Let us bring Him silver and gold.

4. Said the king to the people ev'rywhere,
   Listen to what I say!
   Pray for peace, people ev'rywhere,
   Listen to what I say!
   The Child, the Child, sleeping in the night;
   He will bring us goodness and light,
   He will bring us goodness and light.

YOU'RE ALL I WANT FOR CHRISTMAS

Words and Music by GLEN MOORE
and SEGER ELLIS

Intro

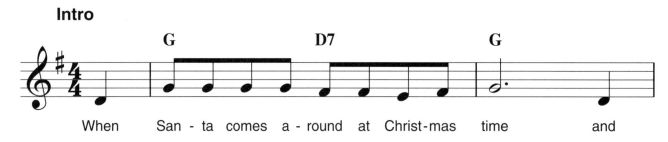

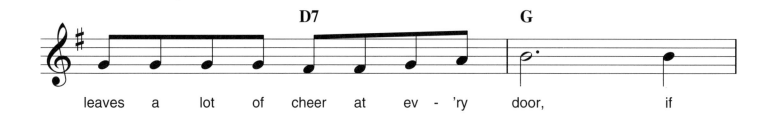

When San - ta comes a - round at Christ - mas time and

leaves a lot of cheer at ev - 'ry door, if

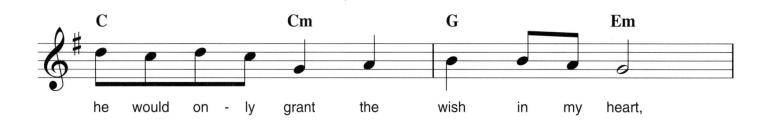

he would on - ly grant the wish in my heart,

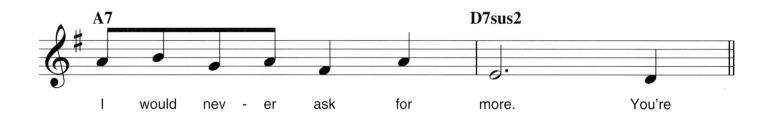

I would nev - er ask for more. You're

Chorus

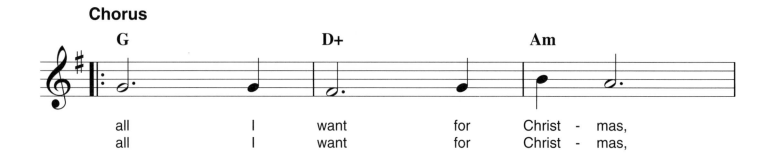

all   I   want   for   Christ - mas,
all   I   want   for   Christ - mas,

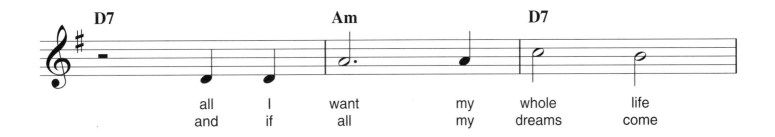

D7 — all / and — I / if — want / all

Am — my / my — whole / dreams

D7 — life / come

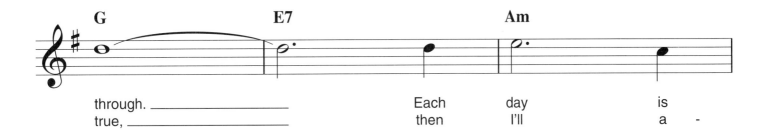

G — through. / true,

E7 — Each / then — day / I'll

Am — is / a -

1.

B7 — just — like — Christ - mas,

Em — an - y

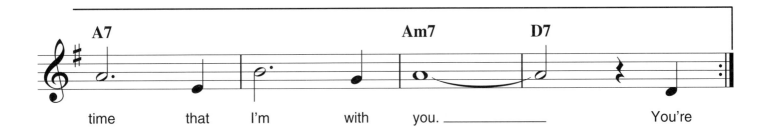

A7 — time — that — I'm — with

Am7 — you.

D7 — You're

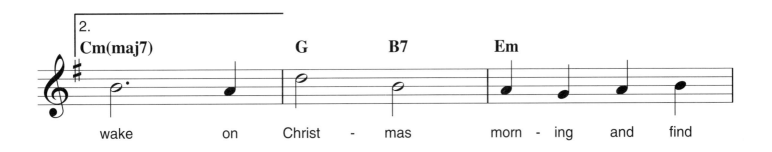

2.

Cm(maj7) — wake — on

G — Christ - mas

B7

Em — morn - ing — and — find

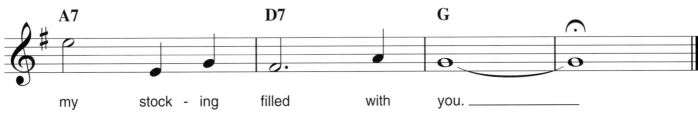

A7 — my — stock - ing

D7 — filled — with — you.

G

LET IT SNOW! LET IT SNOW! LET IT SNOW!

Words by SAMMY CAHN
Music by JULE STYNE

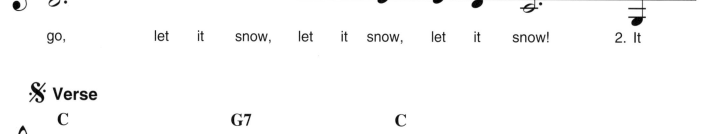

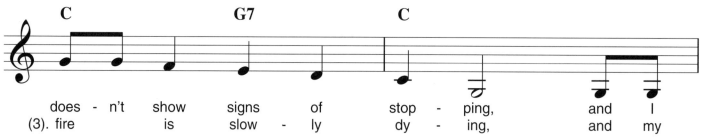

Verse

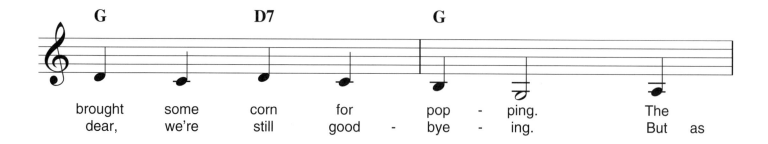

lights are turned way down low, } let it
long as you love me so, }

To Coda ⊕

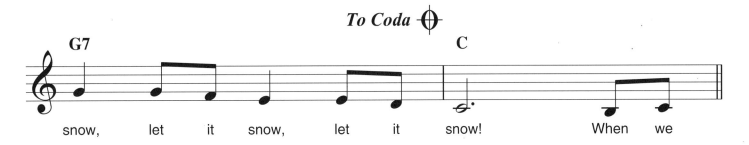

snow, let it snow, let it snow! When we

Bridge

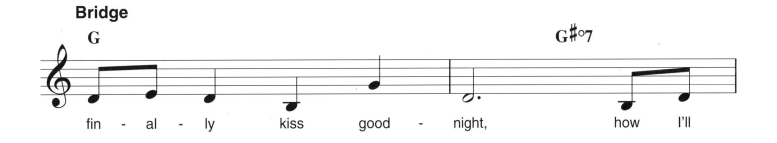

fin - al - ly kiss good - night, how I'll

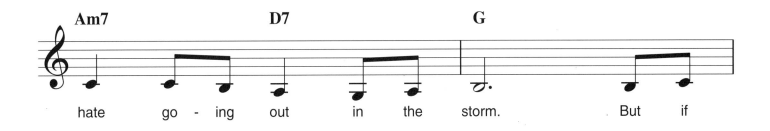

hate go - ing out in the storm. But if

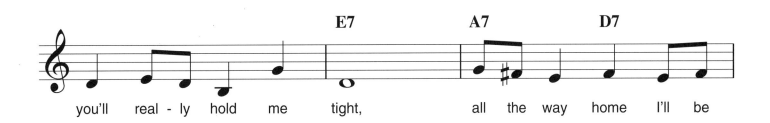

you'll real - ly hold me tight, all the way home I'll be

D.S. al Coda ⊕ **Coda**

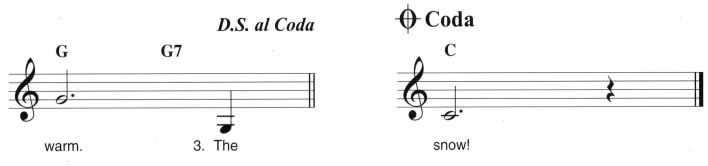

warm. 3. The snow!

SILVER BELLS
from the Paramount Picture THE LEMON DROP KID

Words and Music by JAY LIVINGSTON
and RAY EVANS

1. Cit-y side-walks, bus-y side-walks dressed in
(2.) street lights, e-ven stop-lights blink a

hol-i-day style, in the air there's a feel-ing of Christ-mas.
bright red and green, as the shop-pers rush home with their treas-ures.

Chil-dren laugh-ing, peo-ple pass-ing, meet-ing smile af-ter
Hear the snow crunch, see the kids bunch, this is San-ta's big

smile, and on ev-'ry street cor-ner you'll hear: _____
scene, and a-bove all this bus-tle you'll hear: _____

Chorus

Sil-ver bells, _____ sil-ver bells. _____ It's Christ-mas time in the

cit-y. Ring-a-ling, _____ hear them ring. _____

Soon it will be Christ-mas day. 2. Strings of day. _____

HERE COMES SANTA CLAUS
(RIGHT DOWN SANTA CLAUS LANE)

Words and Music by GENE AUTRY
and OAKLEY HALDEMAN

SANTA CLAUS IS COMIN' TO TOWN

Words by HAVEN GILLESPIE
Music by J. FRED COOTS